NOTEBOOK

BELONGS TO:

PHONE:

E-MAIL:

Printed in Great Britain
by Amazon

87719658R00066